W9-DBX-761

TELL ME WHY, TELL ME HOW

WHY DO LEAVES CHANGE COLOR?

TERRY ALLAN HICKS

 **Marshall Cavendish** Benchmark

New York

Published by Marshall Cavendish Benchmark
An imprint of Marshall Cavendish Corporation

This publication represents the opinions and views of the author based on Terry Allan Hicks's personal experience, knowledge, and research. The information in this book serves as a general guide only. The author and publisher have used their best efforts in preparing this book and disclaim liability rising directly and indirectly from the use and application of this book.

Other Marshall Cavendish Offices:
Marshall Cavendish International (Asia) Private Limited, 1 New Industrial Road, Singapore 536196 • Marshall Cavendish International (Thailand) Co Ltd. 253 Asoke, 12th Flr, Sukhumvit 21 Road, Klongtoey Nua, Wattana, Bangkok 10110, Thailand • Marshall Cavendish (Malaysia) Sdn Bhd, Times Subang, Lot 46, Subang Hi-Tech Industrial Park, Batu Tiga, 40000 Shah Alam, Selangor Darul Ehsan, Malaysia

Marshall Cavendish is a trademark of Times Publishing Limited.

All websites were available and accurate when this book was sent to press.

Library of Congress Cataloging-in-Publication Data
Hicks, Terry Allan.
  Why do leaves change color? / by Terry Allan Hicks. — 1st ed.
      p. cm. — (Tell me why, tell me how)
  Summary: "Provides comprehensive information on the process of how and why
leaves change color"—Provided by publisher.
  Includes index.
  ISBN 978-0-7614-4827-3
  1. Leaves—Color—Juvenile literature. 2. Fall foliage—Juvenile
literature. I. Title. II. Series: Tell me why, tell me how.
  QK649.H53 2010
  575.5'7—dc22
  2009051252

Photo research by Candlepants Incorporated

Cover Photo: Ron and Patty Thomas / Getty Images

The photographs in this book are used by permission and through the courtesy of:
Getty Images: Christopher Robbins, 1; Travelpix Ltd, 5; Tom Mareschal, 7; Wally Eberhart, 8; John Burcham, 10; Jozsef Szentpeteri, 13; Dr. Richard Kessel & Dr. Gene Shih, 14; Jean-Pierre Pieuchot, 16; Andy Caulfield, 22; Cowan Jules, 23. *Alamy Images*: Renee Morris, 4; Gabe Palmer, 20; Chris Fredriksson, 25; travelib prime, 24. *Shutterstock*: 11, 17. *Marshall Cavendish Image Library*: 19.

Editor: Joy Bean
Publisher: Michelle Bisson
Art Director: Anahid Hamparian
Series Designer: Alex Ferrari

Printed in Malaysia (T)
1 3 5 6 4 2

CONTENTS

When spring arrives and the weather begins to warm up, buds start to form on trees. These buds will grow into leaves.

A Sign of the Times

In many parts of the United States and elsewhere in the world, the changing colors of the leaves are a sure sign that the seasons are changing. The pale green **buds** that first appear on trees and other plants in early spring are a welcome indication of warmer weather to come. When the

When a tree's leaves have all changed to a dark green color, it usually means that it is summertime.

mature leaves have turned a deeper, darker green, we know that summer is at its height. And the spectacular colors of autumn—yellow and orange and gold, red and purple and brown—warn us that winter is on its way.

Trees and other forest plants cover close to 15 million

square miles (39 million square kilometers)—more than one-quarter of Earth's land surface. We use their wood for building materials and for fuel. We also use plant matter to make everything from clothing to medications. Far more importantly, the world's trees and other plants produce almost one-third of the **oxygen** we breathe. Without oxygen, life on Earth could not exist. Trees and other land-based plants create oxygen using their leaves, and this process is what makes leaves change color.

Some places—the New England states, for example—are famous for the beauty of their autumn leaves. The leaves there usually begin to change color in mid- to late September. But leaves in other regions show very little color change in the course of a year, even though these areas may be home to billions of trees.

As many as 100,000 different types of trees exist in the world. Most of them fall into two categories. **Coniferous trees**, such as spruces and pines, are the type we see everywhere at Christmastime. They have hard, narrow **needles** instead of leaves, and they produce cones instead of flowers to house their seeds and **pollen**. These trees usually grow in cool or cold **climates**. They keep most of their

Whether a leaf changes color, how much, and even what color it changes to depends on many different factors: what type of tree or plant it is, the part of the world in which it is found, and what the weather conditions are like there.

Coniferous trees, such as this white spruce, have thin needles instead of flat leaves.

needles—and most of their color—all year round. **Deciduous trees** include maples, oaks, and elms and grow across large areas of the United States. They usually have wide, flat leaves, and they always produce flowers. These are the trees whose leaves change color and eventually fall off.

The process through which leaves change color and

eventually fall off their trees is slow and complicated. And before we can discuss why and how it happens, we must talk more about what a leaf is and the role it plays in the life of a tree.

This leaf, on the Hawaiian island of Kauai, is big, but leaves in some other parts of the world can be many times its size.

All About Leaves

The world's leaves come in an amazing variety of sizes, shapes, and structures. Some African raffia palm trees have leaves 65 feet (20 meters) long—almost the length of a New York City subway car! The smallest leaf in the world may belong to the pygmy weed, a wildflower that grows in California. Its leaves are only a little more than one-twentieth of an inch (1.3 millimeters) long. That means one leaf could easily fit on the head of an ordinary straight pin.

Some leaves are sharp and pointed, shaped like swords or spears. Others are round, oval, or even diamond shaped. A maple leaf is shaped almost like a human hand. The leaf of the

One leaf, such as this one from a mountain ash tree, can be made up of many parts.

gingko tree—one of the oldest plants in the world, mostly unchanged for more than 200 million years—looks very much like an old-fashioned lady's fan.

Leaves' structures vary widely, too. Some leaves, such as the familiar oak leaf, are one single piece. But other leaves, including some of the largest of all leaves, have so many parts that they actually look like groups of separate leaves. The placement of the leaves on a tree can also be very different. Some leaves stand alone on a single **stalk** that attaches to the main part of the plant, while others cluster together or spread out along both sides of a stalk.

But no matter what leaves look like, they all have certain things in common. Every leaf has a stalk and a **blade**, a broad surface that captures sunlight. The surface of the blade has tiny openings called **stomata**—much like the pores in your skin—that take in water and air.

A leaf also has a complex network of tubelike veins, which is part of the tree's **vascular system**. This system carries water and **nutrients** throughout the rest of the tree. It brings water from the roots and stem of the tree to the leaves. This water then moves back through the stalks and delivers the food created in the leaves to the rest of the tree. This

This close-up look at a leaf shows the veins that carry water and nutrients.

exchange process is essential to the survival of the tree—and the planet itself.

When the first "veined" plants appeared on Earth, about 425 million years ago, the oxygen content in the air was much lower than it is today. The planet's land surfaces were hot, barren, and rocky, and almost all life was found in the oceans.

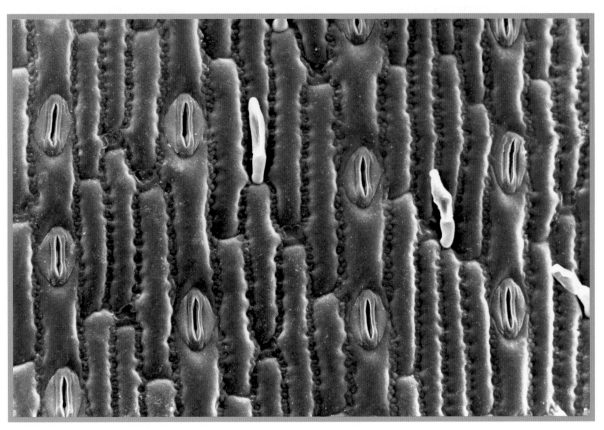

Microscopic pores, called stomata, allow a tree leaf to take in nutrients and air.

It was only after the first of these leafy plants—which were ferns, not trees—began creating more oxygen that the first primitive land animals were able to survive. By the time the first dinosaurs walked the earth, leaves had been hard at work for 140 million years, making the planet a more livable place. They did this, just as they do now, by transforming the basic building blocks of life.

The most important building block of life is a substance called **carbon**. Leaves take in carbon from the air through their stomata in the form of **carbon dioxide**. They also take in water. Trees and other plants turn these two substances into the fuel they need to live and grow. This process occurs inside green leaves. It occurs at a much lower rate in coniferous trees than in deciduous ones, because the narrow surfaces of coniferous needles cannot take in nearly as much carbon. But what is it that makes leaves green—and all those other colors—in the first place?

These green trees and plants contain large amounts of the pigment chlorophyll.

The Colors of Life

Pigments create the colors of trees and plants. Pigments are chemicals found in trees and plants, as well as in almost all other living things. There are three main types of plant pigments. The most important of all is, by far, is **chlorophyll**.

Chlorophyll is the pigment that makes leaves green, but it also has more important duties. Chlorophyll captures the energy in sunlight and uses this energy to create the fuel the tree needs to survive and grow. This process is known as **photosynthesis**. Photosynthesis works by using light to

Chlorophyll needs sunlight to provide trees and other plants with energy.

combine carbon dioxide taken in by the stomata of the leaves with water taken in by the leaves and the roots. The result is a type of sugar called **glucose** that the tree uses as food.

Sunlight causes plants to create more and more chlorophyll. This is why leaves usually become darker and darker green in the summertime, when there is the most light. Chlorophyll is destroyed during the process of photosynthesis, and leaves must constantly create more of this substance. There is so much chlorophyll in leaves in the summertime, in fact, that it is difficult or even impossible to see other pigments in the leaves. But they are there.

The pigments that create the yellow, gold, and orange colors of autumn leaves play a role in photosynthesis by directing sunlight to chlorophyll. These pigments are present in leaves throughout the growing season, but they usually cannot be seen because they are hidden by the green of the chlorophyll. This is partly because there is so much more chlorophyll than other pigments during the growing season. But it is also caused by the fact that green blocks out colors such as yellow and orange.

The pigments that create red, purple, and brown leaves are present only in small amounts during the growing season.

The pigments that create red and yellow colors show through in autumn, but they are in leaves in spring and summer as well.

These pigments are also affected by the weather. When the air begins to turn cooler, leaves make more of the red, purple, and brown pigments.

Chlorophyll, too, is affected by changes in temperature and other weather conditions, but in the opposite way. As the end of summer grows closer, there are fewer and fewer hours of daylight, so there is less and less sunlight.

As the days turn cooler in autumn, more and more brown pigment is created in some leaves.

The leaves produce less chlorophyll, and the chlorophyll that is broken down during photosynthesis is not replaced. Then the other pigments begin to show through. The result is the display of colors we have come to know and love every autumn.

This fir tree in Colorado stays green all year long, but the aspen trees surrounding it turn bright yellow in autumn.

A Leaf Dies, a Tree Lives

The color changes of autumn are not the same everywhere. North America probably has the greatest variety of autumn leaves in the world. This is partly because of its mild climate. North America also has more types of trees than some other parts of the world, such as Europe. Areas where there are also great autumn color changes include Japan, Korea, and other parts of East Asia.

In many parts of North America, autumn brings us the pale yellows and oranges of elms, and the intense red of oaks, all in one place.

Timing and geography help determine the color of leaves. The farther north we go, the sooner the cool weather comes, and the sooner the sunlight fades. This is why leaves may change color in Canada several weeks before they do in the United States. The opposite is true below the **equator**, where the colder zones are farther to the south and the seasons are the opposite of ours.

In many places the leaf colors change very little or not at all. For example, near the equator the leaves of deciduous trees change very little. This is because the amount of sunlight reaching these regions remains almost constant throughout the year. So a lot of chlorophyll is made, and the colors of other pigments are hidden.

As the display of autumn colors is taking place, the tree is

As winter approaches, leaves become brittle as their veins close up.

The word *fall*, which we sometimes use in place of *autumn*, is a reference to the falling of the leaves.

preparing for another essential part of its life cycle—the falling of the leaves.

The leaves of a deciduous tree fall because they are too delicate to survive harsh winter conditions. When photosynthesis stops and glucose is no longer produced, the veins close up, and the leaves and their stalks dry up. This makes the leaves fragile and brittle. Eventually, the stalks break,

Now I Know!

Why do leaves in tropical zones not change color very much?

The amount of sunlight they receive remains almost the same throughout the year, so they keep producing chlorophyll.

and the leaves fall to the ground. But even these now-dead leaves do not go to waste. They break down, and the matter in them provides the soil with nutrients that will be used by other trees and plants. They also create a layer on the forest floor that both holds rainwater and protects the roots of other trees. Even after they fall, the leaves are helping to prepare for the next phase in the life cycle of the tree. In spring, green buds will become the tree's new set of leaves, beginning the life cycle all over again.

 Activity

Leaves are constantly changing, but you can preserve their beauty for a long time by coating them in wax with the help of an electric iron. Get an adult to help you with the iron.

WHAT YOU WILL NEED:

- Some leaves you have gathered. They can be any type of leaves from any time of year. If you use autumn leaves, make sure they are not too dry or they might crumble.
- An iron and an ironing board or table
- An old piece of cloth (for example, a towel)
- Two sheets of waxed paper

WHAT TO DO

1. Place the cloth on the ironing board or table. Lay one sheet of waxed paper on the cloth. Place the leaves on the waxed paper. Then cover them with the other sheet of waxed paper. After that, cover both the leaves and waxed paper with an old cloth or towel.

2. Now, with an adult's help, heat the iron—it does not need to be very hot, and steam is not necessary—and use it to carefully press down on the leaves through the cloth and waxed paper.

3. Lift up the top layer of waxed paper, and you will find that the heat and pressure of the iron have coated the leaves with wax and sealed in their shape and color. If you keep them in a safe place, such as a picture frame, they should last for many years. To press more leaves, use new sheets of waxed paper, because the sheets lose much of their waxy coating with each use.

 Glossary

blade—The broad, often flat part of the leaf of a deciduous plant.

bud—The first spring outgrowth of a plant, which may become a leaf or flower.

carbon—A basic building block found in all living things.

carbon dioxide—One of the main components of air.

chlorophyll—A green pigment that plays a role in photosynthesis.

climate—The average temperature and weather conditions in a particular area.

coniferous tree—A tree that has sharp needles instead of broad leaves and that produces cones instead of flowers.

deciduous (also called broad-leaved) tree—A tree that has broad, often flat leaves and produces flowers.

equator—An imaginary line around the center of Earth that divides it into northern and southern halves.

glucose—A type of sugar that plants and other living things use as food.

mature—Fully grown.

needle—A thin, sharp leaf that grows on a coniferous tree.

nutrient—A substance that allows a living thing to live and grow.

oxygen—An element that is found in air and is necessary for the survival of most forms of life.

photosynthesis—A chemical process in plants that uses light to produce energy.

pigment—A substance that creates color.

pollen—A substance created by plants that plays a role in reproduction.

stalk (also called a stem)—The slender part of a leaf that attaches it to the main part of a plant.

stomata—Openings in the surface of a leaf that take in air and water.

vascular system—The network of tube-like veins that transports water and nutrients throughout a plant.

 Find Out More

BOOKS

Burnie, David. *Tree* (DK Eyewitness Books). New York: Dorling Kindersley, 2005.

René, Ellen. *Investigating Why Leaves Change Their Color*. New York: Rosen
    Publishing, 2009.

Smith, Charles W. G. *Fall Foliage: The Mystery, Science, and Folklore of Autumn
    Leaves*. Guilford, CT: The Globe Pequot Press, 2005.

WEBSITES

Autumn Colors—How Leaves Change Color

www.na.fs.fed.us/spfo/pubs/misc/autumn/autumn_colors.htm

Autumn Leaf Color: Why Do Leaves Change Color in the Fall?

www.sciencemadesimple.com/leaves.html

E-Center: Why Leaves Change Color

www.esf.edu/pubprog/brochure/leaves/leaves.htm

Index

Page numbers in **boldface** are illustrations.